Dialogues with God

Books by Frances J. Roberts

Make Haste, My Beloved
A tender but insistent call from the heart of God to the heart of His people. It is a call to purity: a light illuminating our path. A book you will read today and keep forever.

Come Away, My Beloved
This book will help you find the quiet place of communion. sense the presence of God and respond to His overtures. A six-part compilation of the six booklets listed below.

Booklets:
Lovest Thou Me?
Living Water
Launch Out!
Learn to Reign
Listen to the Silence
The Sounding of the Trumpet

When the Latch Is Lifted
A delightful gift book of heartwarming poetry. Illustrated.

Progress of Another Pilgrim
Challenging, inspirational. A thrilling sequel to "Come Away. My Beloved" and "Dialogues with God."

Dialogues with God
Devotional writings. Similar to "Come Away My Beloved."

On the Highroad of Surrender
A choice spiritual feast awaits you in this book which plumbs the depths and scales the heights of divine revelation. Inspiring and practical.

Angel in the Fire
A beautiful book on death, grief and eternal life. Gift quality, with four full page pictorial illustrations.

Total Love
Frances J. Roberts' latest book. A rich treasury of spiritual insights.

MUSIC

O Wondrous Love
A long-play stereo record of ten beautiful songs with words and music by Frances J. Roberts.

Published by KING'S FARSPAN, INC.
1473 S. La Luna Ave.. Ojai. California 93023

Dialogues with God

FRANCES J. ROBERTS

KING'S FARSPAN, INC.
1473 So. La Luna Avenue
Ojai, California 93023

Hardcover edition: ISBN 0-932814-07-7
Softcover edition: ISBN 0-932814-08-5

ILLUSTRATED BY HELEN TWENTYMAN

To Dorothy

FOREWORD

DIALOGUES WITH GOD has grown out of the devotional experiences of the writer. The prayers and responses as received were not captured by the pen primarily with the intention of publication, but were recorded in obedience to the prompting of the Holy Spirit, for the purpose of enlightenment.

Words from Isaiah 50:4 became a deep prayer in my heart and a motivating influence. "Waken me morning by morning, waken my ear to hear as a learner." Out of this desire has grown a communication with God of which the writings of this book are a part.

Through faith in the Lord Jesus Christ we are brought into God's family. Through the indwelling Holy Spirit the power to live this new life begins to be manifested. But only through faithful and continual *communion* do we grow in grace and receive illumination to bring us into fuller comprehension of deeper truth. Only as we look to Him daily to teach us are we strengthened in faith. Only as we seek His face and study His word do we learn in the Spirit the mysteries of the Kingdom.

As a vehicle of worship, may this book implement your prayer life and help to open the door of your inmost soul to the breath of God and to the compassionate heart of the Lord Jesus Christ.

O my dove, that art in the clefts of the rock, in the secret places of the stairs, let me see thy countenance, let me hear thy voice; for sweet is thy voice, and thy countenance is comely.

Song of Solomon 2:14

Sit Thou Upon the Throne

Lord God of Hosts, Thou Who dwellest between the cherubim, Thou who hast taken up Thine abode within my heart; give ear to my cry, yea, turn not away when I call upon Thee. O Holy Father, righteous in all Thy ways and just in all Thy dealings, forgive my sins and pardon mine iniquities and cleanse Thou my heart from secret faults.

For Thou art mindful of the needs of Thy children, and Thou art gracious and tenderhearted. Thou art ready to forgive. Thou dost move to make reconciliation before we call. Thou art watching for the return of the backslider ere he set foot on the road home.

Blessed be Thy Name! Marvelous is Thy compassion, and Thy thoughts toward me have been thoughts of pity and kindness. Praise shall be my meat and drink.

Sit Thou upon the throne of my heart and rule my affections; for to do Thy will is my supreme desire and in keeping Thy commandments my soul delights.

My Word Thy Strength

Make straight paths for thy feet lest in time of weakness ye be turned aside, lest in a place of decision ye be led in the wrong direction. But if ye walk circumspectly and in the light of My Word, ye shall know plainly, and if ye look to Me I will guide thee with Mine eye. Yea, I will watch over thee in love. I will bless thee with My bounty.

My presence shall go with thee, keeping thee in peace, and goodness and mercy shall follow thee. My song shalt thou hear in the night, and My Word shall be thy strength. I will deliver thee from the evil one and I will undergird thee with My faithfulness.

Thou shalt walk upon high places because of the Lord thy God, for in Him is might and power and He will perfect that which concerneth thee. Yea, He will keep thee in all thy ways.

Psalm
of
Praise

O the depth of the riches both of the wisdom and knowledge of God. How unsearchable are His mercies, and His ways past finding out.

> For He found me in a waste-howling wilderness;
> He led me by His hand; He brought me out; yea,
> He hath brought me into a large place.
> He set His love upon me, and
> caused His face to shine upon me.

He showered upon me the dews of heaven and made my way as a path of light.

He made His angels ministers of mercy.

> He put His words in my mouth,
> and His speech has been upon me.
> Yea, He hath come as a flood.
> With torrents of blessing He caused my heart to overflow.

Surely, in the daytime

> He hath been as an encompassing cloud,

and in the nighttime

> His Spirit hath illuminated the darkness as a fiery pillar.

Yea, in Thy presence darkness fleeth away,

> faith is swallowed up in sight,
> and doubt is dispelled as hoar frost before sunlight.
> Heaven is Thy throne, and earth is Thy footstool,

yet hast Thou deigned to make Thine abode within

> tabernacles of clay!

This thought is too great for me, and how can my heart
        receive it?
That Thou art preparing heavenly mansions for my habitation,
    this my mind can understand.
But that Thou, the Almighty God
        Who filleth and ordereth the vast universe of earth
        and of heaven,
should stoop to fill my frail cup with Thy divine effulgence —
    this delights my soul, —
    but my thoughts cannot grasp it.

Living Stones –

        Lo, I have set Eternity in thine heart.
        Yea, I have made thee to be a LIVING STONE.
For the Almighty delighteth not to dwell in temples made with
hands. Lo, saith the Lord,
        I will build Me an house and fashion it with lively stones.
        Yea, I will build My Church and found it upon the Rock;
        and the gates of Hell shall not prevail against it,
neither shall one stone be removed out of its place.
        For I will dwell in the midst of My people
        and I will be glorified in them.

The Spirit of Wisdom

As the Holy Spirit giveth thee utterance, so shall ye speak. For ye shall not speak anything of thyself, but ye shall speak as it is given unto thee. And thou shalt know that it is from the hand of God that ye have received the message. For who has known His mind, and who has understood His thoughts? They are higher than the heavens are above the earth. Who can understand? Even as Jesus Himself said: there are some things that only the Father knoweth.

But He has given the Spirit of wisdom and understanding in the knowledge of Him, to the end that ye may come to know Him. Therefore He saith: Lean not unto thine own understanding, for the wisdom of the wise is but to perish, but the knowledge of God is of eternal proportion.

Therefore, come unto Me in humbleness of mind, and with meekness receive ye the ingrafted Word which is able to make thee wise unto thine eternal salvation.

By My Word is thy sanctification accomplished; for it is written: *Without holiness no man shall see the Lord.* This is both present and future — both in this present world and in that which is to come. And if thine eye be single and thy heart pure, thy whole being will be radiant with divine revelation.

So shall thine understanding be deepened and thy vision broadened.

The Inheritance of the Saints

O Lord, My God, I have heard of Thee by the hearing of the ear, but I long to see Thee. Yea, I desire to behold Thee DAILY in the light of fresh revelation, yea, by the illumination of the Spirit who dwelleth within. I need the daily inward strengthening of the new man in the power of Thy might, that I may be enabled to walk in obedience to Thy divine commands.

For if we WALK according to Thy divine revelation, we shall enjoy Thy fellowship and presence; but if the light that is in us becomes darkness by our disobedience, how great is our darkness! How helpless our plight!

For we know to do good — we are aware of our obligation — but we continually battle the tendencies of our human natures to do otherwise. For the flesh resisteth the progress of the Spirit. (Rom. 7:15-25) But as Paul, we make our confession: *Thanks be unto God Who giveth us the victory through our Lord Jesus Christ!*

Make me to WILL to do Thy will, and show me plainly the path of Thy choosing. Let me walk in harmony with Thee — neither run ahead nor question. For I know Thee, that all Thy ways are righteousness, and all Thy paths are peace. Thy song is a song of joy. Thy steps are sure, and Thy way is a way of victory. Thou hast triumphed over all Thy foes. Thou shalt overthrow the thrones of the mighty, but Thou crownest the righteous with glory. Thy kingdom shall be forever and ever, an everlasting kingdom that shall never be cut off. This is the inheritance of the saints, and the promise to them that serve Thee.

And we know that the present conflict shall be counted trivial in the light of the mighty triumph that is to come. For they shall stand before Thee — all the dead both small and great, to be judged by those things which are written in the books: but he that believeth in the Son hath everlasting life, and shall not come into condemnation, but is passed already from death into life. (Jno. 5:24) These who believe shall reign with Thee, yea, they shall judge both men and angels.

Small wonder the writer of the letter to the Hebrews called this "so great salvation"! For the more we ponder its magnitude, the more it passeth human comprehension, and to express it exhausteth the powers of speech.

Let me hearken to Thy words in John 15, and simply abide in Thee as the branch in the vine. Make this present moment one of victory in Thee, and let me live moment by moment, lost in Thy love.

We Look
to Thee

O blessed Saviour,
    to Thee we pour out our praise—
    at Thy feet we fall to worship.
    Thy Name shall be upon our lips
    and Thy song in our mouths.
We look not upon things seen, but upon that which faith produces,
    for that which we see is perishing
    but that which is of faith is eternal.
We look to Thee for victories in the Spirit.
We look to Thee for grace to bear the yoke with willing hearts.
Yea, we look to Thee to be our fountain of rejoicing;
    for whatever betide, Thou changest not,
    nor canst Thou ever fail.
    Thy presence fills our cup with joy.
    Thy peace stills every storm.
In Thy Name is the balm of Gilead. Thy love knoweth no bounds.
    Let us be lost in Thy fulness.

One Ambition –

O My child,
    'There is a place of quiet rest,
        Near to the heart of God.
    A place where sin cannot molest,
        Near to the heart of God.'
                —McAfee

Come. Come often.
Come seeking. Come needing.
Wait not until ye may bring Me a gift.
Come because ye love Me.
Come knowing that I have loved thee first,
even while ye were yet in trespasses and sins.
Come asking no questions.
Come speaking no words.
Come because I love you.
Come because I desire thy fellowship
more than thou canst know.
Ye seek to serve Me,
and fret because of thy limited service.
No . . . no . . . no.
Can ye never learn the lesson I sought to teach Martha?
Can ye never be content to sit as Mary?
Better thy feet were cut off
than that they carry thee outside the circle of communion.
Ye consider the usefulness of thy life.
Thou shouldst have but one ambition —
to love Me and to be near Me.
Let Me take care of all the rest.
Let Me arrange the pattern of thy life.
Let Me direct thy service,
and it shall be not a service of dead works and self-effort,
but an overflow of divine love.
This is My Father's work.
I do not require and have not requested thy work.
Nay, but ye become a hindrance
when ye set about to work for Me thus.
Set thy heart to be near Me. Live close to My heart.
Look upon My face.
I will satisfy thee completely.
I will keep thee from anxiety.
I will heal all thy diseases.
I will cause My face to shine upon thee,
and thou shalt be glad.

This Is the Glory Life

Behold, I say unto thee, *This is the way, walk ye in it,*
     neither turn to the right hand nor to the left.
For I shall make the path for thy feet a plain path,
     and light shall be there,
     and there shall be the shining of My glory.
It shall not be the glory of man. It shall be the glory of God.
For My thoughts are not your thoughts, neither are your ways
     My ways,
     saith the Lord. (Isa. 55:8)
Therefore, lean upon Me for wisdom, yea, lean wholly upon Me,
     for thou knowest not the direction of thyself, but it shall be
     revealed unto thee by My Spirit, saith the Lord.
Day by day and step by step, thou shalt walk by faith,
     not by thine own cunningly devised plans.
I desire to do a new thing. How canst thou discover it?
If thou couldst, thou wouldst spoil the thrill of it,
     as a child finding his gift before the time.
Question Me not, nor ask Me why,
     neither put confidence in the wisdom of thine own thoughts.
Thou grievest My Spirit.
     Thou hinderest My plans for thee.
     Thou delayest My purpose.
     Thou art causing suffering to thyself and others.

What human wisdom could have anticipated Calvary?
Indeed, who could have anticipated the details of Bethlehem?
This is the meaning of My command that thou shouldst delight in
      MY ways.
    This is the glory life.
This is the new, fresh, vibrant, thrilling wonder of God
    living within man.
    All thou doest otherwise, thou controllest thyself;
      but learn in this to be fully controlled by My Spirit.
I will never fail thee nor lead thee astray.
I will accomplish that which I purpose.

Forgive My Questions

O Blessed Jesus, this is not the way of the flesh
    but the way of the Spirit.
Remove every hindering thing.
I ask Thee not to answer my questions but to forgive them.
    I ask Thee not so much for strength as for a pure heart.
For when I acknowledge my weakness, then I experience Thy
    strength, but when I would walk in my own wisdom,
      I am not only weak, but sinful through disobedience.
    It is written, 'To obey is better than sacrifice'.
O God, give me strength to obey!

Seek the
Fresh
Anointing

Open thine heart to Me
    and I will pour in fragrant oil.
Lift to Me thy cup
    and I will fill it to overflowing with the waters of life.
Bring to Me all thy need
    and I will supply abundantly out of My fulness.
I am not a man that I should be limited,
    but I long to give and to give again and again.
This is not a matter of My granting to thee one great supply
    to be stored and used little by little as needed,
but I give to you a fresh outpouring as each need arises —
    yea, and BEFORE the need arises
that ye may be prepared in advance
and that in each emergency ye may have no lack.
I give to thee in order that ye may serve Me
    as a channel of blessing to others.
I know those who shall come,
and I know the specific need of each individual case,
    and thus I give you exactly what will be suitable for each one.
So be diligent to come,
    for why should I send anyone unto thee if ye are not
        prepared?
And if ye be prepared, I will not fail to send to thee the very ones
    for whom I have made the provision.
Ye need not seek them out.
    How, verily, canst thou know?
But I Myself shall send whom I choose
    and thou shalt marvel.

Thus shall ye surely know that this is My work —
  yea, the work of God the Father.
  This is not "serving Jesus" in the popular approach
    to so-called "Christian work".
This is the doing of the will of God.
  As it is written,
He that doeth the will of God abideth forever. I Jno. 2:17
  Service to Me by the will of the flesh is temporal,
  but the doing of the will of God is eternal.
And this is the will of God, that ye be about the Father's business—
  that ye work the works of Him that hath called thee
  and now sends thee, even as did Jesus when He walked
    among men.
Leave all else to Me.
Seek the fresh anointing
  and I will do the rest.

Reciprocal Action

Blessed be Thy Name forever!
Surely Thy yoke is easy and Thy burden is light.
  No wonder Christ could say as we also may,
"I delight to do Thy will, O God."
  What sheer joy is this to simply expose the interior
    and exterior of the soul to the glory of God
  and let Him do all the arranging of circumstances!
It is like being a tree
  and simply allowing the roots to remain planted,
and drinking in God's gifts of sunshine and rain,
and just watching the fruit grow and mature —
  silently, miraculously,
  untouched by any but the hand of God.
Blessed privilege!
Blessed provision for the hungry passer-by.
  There is no loss to the tree if its fruit is gathered.
  There would be only needless waste if it were not so.
But God's purposes are fulfilled in the reciprocal action—
  producing the fruit on the one hand,
  and sending the hungry to partake of it on the other hand.

Nor has the tree any choice in this matter.
>It possesses no power to discriminate or eliminate,
>and there is no possibility of self-preservation.

The fruit is produced by the will of the Creator
and the fruit is partaken of by the will of the recipient.
>Even so,

all that God produces by His Spirit in thy life
He shall, by His sovereign will, make available
>to those of His own choice
>and to those of a hungry heart.

Many there are of hungry heart who bear a cheerful countenance.
Many there are who suffer poverty of soul whilst they enjoy
>the luxuries of this present world.

Man seeth only the outward appearance,
>but the inner state of the soul is open to the scrutiny
>of the Almighty.

Blessed joy thus to be co-laborers with Him,
>'working out' to others as He 'worketh in' us
>to do all His good pleasure.

Praise of the Infinite

O My child, the heavens are filled with songs of praise, and above the tumult of a decadent world, I hear the sweet music of the prayers and hymns of My people.

Before the world began . . . before the creation of human life, the morning stars sang together in a great pean of praise. As a mighty organ, the planets were as an instrument in the hands of the Almighty Creator God, expressing the very joy of His heart. Selah!

*   *   *

The Essence of the Infinite

Praise is the very essence of the Infinite. Faith — that is, its positive, confident, active power, is at one with divine Omnipotence.

So fill our hearts with this priceless grace that we shall be moved by Thy Spirit in acts of faith — to heal the sick, to lift the fallen, to inspire fresh hope in those who despair, to impart a vitalizing sense of Thy love to the friendless, and encouragement to Thy weary faithful servants.

O build up Thy Church in spiritual energy by this interflowing of the power of Thy Spirit, ministering thus to the mutual benefit of the entire Body; that love may prevail among us, and that God may be glorified in our midst, to the sanctification of the whole.

Remember Thy Covenant

O my God, lift the mist that has gathered between.
    Let no foreboding thought intervene.
Do for me all I cannot do for myself
and restore unto me the joy of Thy salvation.
Give me of Thy free Spirit.
    Let no bondage overtake me.
For I have sought to follow Thee.
    I have desired to do Thy will.
Let me yet see the fruit.
    Let not your people die in the wilderness.
        Yea, let my life be taken from me,
        but spare Thy Church for the sake of Thy Name,
        for the sake of Thy testimony.
    Remove not the candlestick. (Rev. 2:5)
Deal in mercy and be patient still,
    even as Thou hast dealt with me.
        Surely as Thou saidst of Israel,
        Thou canst well say of Thy Church,
        "I am married to a back-slider." (Jer. 3:14)
But remember Thy covenant. Remember Thy commandments.
    What God hath joined together let not man put asunder.
Yea, how canst Thou desert Thine own? Surely not . . .
    But though the wheat and the tares grow together,
    cast not away the wheat.
Spare, O God, not because we deserve mercy,
    but because we are Thine own,
        yea, and not only Thy Bride, but Thy Body.
Look upon us tenderly in spite of our lack.

I Will Build Up the Walls

Lo, I have drawn thee out of many waters.
 I have preserved thy life from destruction.
 I have kept thy foot that it hath not slipped.
 I have kept My promise and fulfilled My purpose.
For I have not called thee in vain.
 I have not put My Spirit upon thee to any idle end.
But I have been thy shield and buckler and I Myself thine exceed-
  ing great reward.
 For I am the Reward of them that seek Me—
  and as a man seeketh, so he findeth.
Thou hast sought Me with thy whole heart
 and thou hast found Me amply sufficient.
Did I at any time fail thee?
 Hast thou at any time lifted thine hand for the task appointed
  that I have not sent My power?
 Hast thou spoken and I have not answered,
 or cried and I have not heard?
Nay. But simultaneously we have worked.
 For so is the operation of the Spirit
  that with every command issued,
  even so is the power supplied.
Then rejoice!
 Look not upon what might have been,
 but praise Me for that which has been accomplished.
Praise Me and exercise faith.
 So shall I make each and every seed sown to flourish
 and shall give a glorious rich harvest.
O magnify My Name.
Let thy countenance be glad.
 Let thine heart be lifted up in song,
for I am the Mighty Conqueror.
 I will make the light to shine,
  and nothing shall stand before Me.
I will remove the stumbling blocks:
 yea, I will place them where they belong
 and I shall build up the walls,

and that which was broken down and scattered shall I restore.
  Yea, for My name's sake and for My people's sake
    which have cried unto Me,
I will not cast off forever; but I will gather thee
  and I will make thy windows of agates
    and all thy borders of pleasant stones. (Isa. 54:12)
And I will stand in the midst.
Comfort ye, comfort ye My people,
  saith the Lord.
Speak ye words of comfort to My people.
  For He lifteth up the fallen,
  He bindeth up the bruised.
  The broken shall be healed, and the pleasure of the Lord
    shall prosper in His hand.
  Thou shalt surely see of the travail of thy soul
and thou shalt be comforted.

Turn Not Back

Behold, what vistas await thee! For thou hast but passed the threshold. Yea, what glory lies ahead! Turn not back now, neither be discouraged by the steepness of the way, for I am, and shall ever be, at thy side to encourage thee.

Yea, I said, I shall encourage thee. Look not to others for this encouragement; for the aid of man is a fickle thing. Today one may stand with thee, and tomorrow two may stand against thee. And what does it matter? Stood not I Myself alone? Shall the servant expect more kindness than his Master received? Nay, but I say unto thee, though all others forsake thee, yet shall I never fail. This I promise thee, not as Peter who boasted of his loyalty in the flesh, for My promise is founded on the immutability of My eternal word.

So take no thought for thyself — neither thy way nor thy safety, for I have prepared thy path and I will be thy life and thy strength. Couldst thou choose a better way? Shall I leave thee rather to thine own devices? Wouldst thou dare presume to make thine own plans?

* * *

There Is No Second Prize

No! O Lord God, Thou knowest my desire! Thou knowest my heart! Thou knowest that I love Thee. Thou knowest I have no ambitions of my own. I have but one goal, and that goal is

God. I have but one aim, and that to win the prize. Yea, I have but one course to run: that which Thou Thyself hast set before me. I dare not choose another. Banish forever the thought! Rebuke any suggestion from the enemy. Let me follow in the prints of Thy pierced feet. Let me walk with my hand clasped in Thy nail-scarred hand. Let me feel Thine arms about me and my head upon thy shoulder, and what matters then the darkness of the night?

Yea, and there shall of certainty be sunny days. For the shadowy canyon leadeth up to the broad meadow, and the testing days precede the triumphs, but the triumphs SHALL come if we turn not back in the times of testings. For he that goeth on in spite of pain shall surely reap the precious grain. As the scripture saith, "He that goeth forth and weepeth, bearing precious seed shall doubtless come again with rejoicing, bringing his sheaves with him." (Psa. 126:6)

O my God, let me not turn coward. Let me not look to shorten the course. Let me not spare my energies nor seek to keep a reserve of power. For there is for each individual but ONE prize. There is no second prize. Either we win or we become a castaway. (I Cor. 9:24-27) Surely this is not an idle warning. Burn it on our souls. Let the weight of it lie upon our hearts. Let us gird up our minds. Let us be sober and diligent, lest after having witnessed to others we should ourselves become disqualified.

For weeping may endure for a moment, but joy cometh in the morning. Yea, and if we be willing to endure the hardness as good soldiers, we shall only then be accounted worthy to receive a reward in the day of victory.

Who Can Stand Before Thee?

Lord God, Thou fillest the heavens with Thy majesty, and the earth with Thy train. Thou bowest Thyself and comest down. Thou ridest upon the chariot of the wind. Thou bringest forth Thy glory out of the closet of eternity for the eye of man to behold. O Lord, who can stand before Thee? Thou goest forth as the sun — terrible in brightness and magnificent in power.

Lay Thy hand upon my mouth, for who can speak in Thy presence? Great and Wonderful is Thy Name, and Thou fillest heaven and earth.

My Love Is Coexistent with My Power

O My child, I know thy frame and remember that thou art dust, for thus I fashioned thee. But is it not also written that I breathed upon man, and he became a living soul? Said I not that I made him in Mine own image and likeness? Yea, within the house of clay did I place a part of Myself, and each part is equal to the whole. Yea, and one day the earthly tabernacles shall be put off, and we shall be one body, clothed upon with immortality. And without thee would My body be incomplete.

Draw near to My heart; for My love for thee is coexistent with My power. Lo, it is written: Humble thyself under the mighty hand of God and He will lift thee up. (I Pet. 5:6) Yea, e'er thy face touch the dust, I have put Mine arms about thee to draw thee unto My heart.

Yea, I was not in the wind nor the earthquake, but the still small voice. Though the very atmosphere seemeth to move out as I move in, and though the earth tremble beneath My feet, these are but manifestations of My presence.

Thou shalt find Me in the still small voice: It is the love call of My heart.

God is love; and he that dwelleth in love dwelleth in God.
(I Jno. 4:16)

Happy
Art
Thou

Hast thou heard My voice;
hast thou seen My face;
hast thou felt the touch of My hand?
   Walked thou at My side?
   Sattest thou at My feet to be taught of Me?
   Hast thou gone on a mission of mercy under My direction?
Happy art thou; yea, blest beyond all human joy
         that the things of the world could ever bring to thee.
For the joy of following Me,
the joy of serving Me,
and the joy of fellowshipping with Me
         outstrips every other possible pleasure.
At My right hand there are pleasures forevermore. (Psa. 16:11)
   Yea, this speaketh not only of heaven, but of this present
      time, if thy life is hid with Christ in God.
   'Joys are flowing like a river, since the Comforter has come',
      wrote the poet.
My joy becometh thy joy as we labor and live together
         in union and in communion;
   and I rejoice in thee and ye rejoice in Me.
Joy beyond the power to tell!

Glorious Prospect!

Yes, My Father, Heaven alone shall tell the story. And will not one of the thrills of heaven be the recounting of the wondrous workings of Thy hand during our earthly sojourn? Surely there we shall see more clearly how Thou hast wrought in our behalf than we can possibly know at this present time. So much is hid from us now, and well that it is! But there we shall have the complete picture.

Imagine Job seeing for the first time the true meaning behind all his sufferings and losses! Imagine Paul comprehending the full extent and outgrowth of his apostolic ministry's endeavors! And imagine David Livingstone beholding the great victories of missionary enterprise in the continent of Africa; and the martyrs the triumphs of the Church as it grew from the seeds of their sacrifices.

Surely a portion of the happy surprises of the next world will be the fuller knowledge of the meaning and outreach of our present lives in relation to Thy great purposes as they are at work in us even now.

Glorious prospect! Encouraging thought! How we should serve with greater zeal and renewed energy and encouraged faith!

*   *   *

Kindle Anew My Zeal

O my Blessed Heavenly Father, gather me to Thy bosom nor let me ever again wander from Thy nearness. Cast Thy cloak about me, for apart from Thee there is no warmth. There is nothing but aloneness except for Thy reality. Friends may be kind and loved ones dear, but only Thou art the Giver of Life. Only Thou art able to nourish the soul. Only Thou art able to lift the weariness, to implant faith, to refresh and renew the worn and tired spirit. Only Thou canst give light to the mind and guidance for the earthly pathway.

O God, only Thou canst forgive sin and impart righteousness, and what sin is greater than failure to come to Thee with every need, to seek Thine answer to every question, to bring Thee daily the fresh ardor of a devoted heart!

Kindle anew my zeal. Unloose the fountain of tears. Let me never love Thee less than at any moment in the past. Let me not be content to rest upon memories, but do Thou for me a new thing THIS day. Speak a fresh word THIS day and give me a special portion of Thine affection; otherwise I shall be ill-prepared to meet the demand of others.

Rock of Ages

I have not forsaken thee, nor am I far away. Nay, my child, but I am as a Great Rock and ye have been, as it were, looking at the shadow. For I have purposed to be a shelter from sun and storm. But ye have focused your attention on the darkness of the shadow rather than casting thyself upon Me, the Rock. I am not a rock of stone — but I am a Rock of refuge — a powerful protection, a mighty help, a never-failing saviour. My love is as a river with constant supply. *Plenteous grace with Me is found: Grace to pardon all thy sin!*

> *Rock of ages, cleft for me,*
> *Let me hide myself in Thee;*
> *Let the water and the blood,*
> *From Thy riven side which flowed,*
>
> *Be of sin the double cure,*
> *Cleanse from guilt and make me pure.*

—*Toplady*

Vivid
Relationship

Wonderful Saviour! Blessed, holy sacrificial Lamb of God! What depth of love Thou hast demonstrated for us through Thy vicarious death on Calvary; and in Thy resurrection, what sublime victory! What dynamic power was revealed in Thine ascension, what promise of life to come, of ultimate triumph, of complete deliverance from this present world, from suffering and shame — sin and death.

We need to give more thought to Thine ASCENSION than we have been wont to do; *for in Thine ascension we have the two-fold inspiration of Thy complete triumph and glorification, and of the precious promise of Thy bodily return.*

Lo, what great hope is set before us! Yea, what glory; what rapture — what a mighty deliverance — what victory! Let Satan do his worst: Christ has overcome. And He shall tread the wine-press of the fierceness of the wrath of God. (Rev. 19:15) Yea, and the Stone, cut without hands from the mountain, shall be cast at the feet of the image, and He shall utterly cut off the nations in their vanity and in their rebellion, and He shall reign forever and ever. For He shall sit upon the throne of David. His sceptre shall not depart out of His hand; and we shall reign with Him in power and great glory. (Gen. 49:10)

O God, set up Thy kingdom even *now* in our hearts! Let Thy glory be manifested even as it was manifested through the early Church and through consecrated individuals down through the centuries. Let us recapture again, in the face of a luxury-laden, pleasure-seeking, self-loving generation, something of the sacrificial, self-denying, Spirit-empowered devotion evidenced in the lives of such men as Stephen and Paul and Barnabas, and the Beloved John prophesying from the barren shores of Patmos; exiled from friends and fellowship, but "in the Spirit on the Lord's day", seeing the beatific vision of the Son of God.

O God, our hearts cry out to Thee for such living reality, such exquisite closeness, such vivid relationship to Thyself, such a keenness of listening to Thy voice. Capture Thou our hearts. Fire our consecrated imaginations. Sustain us in a holy silence until we hear Thy voice clearly as every other sound is shut out.

We want a message from Thee with fresh impact. We have no desire to be left to our own devices, nor to be forced to lean upon others or depend upon their word. Only what comes to us directly from Thee or from Thine inspired Word will satisfy our hearts. We thank Thee for the inspiration of Christian fellowship; for the stimulation derived from the testimonies of others; for the mutual\blessing and edification of group Bible study; but let us not stop there. Grant us the full enjoyment of the benefits of the Christian community, and to these joys may we add the yet more sacred exercise of private communion and worship: having locked the door, to seek Thy face in the sweet sanctity of solitude, listening to Thy voice as one who listens to the voices of nature on some majestic mountain top.

Magnificent Gift

O My child, I long with a continual desire to draw thee close to My heart. I feel the need of thee, even as ye have need of Me. I cannot be perfectly happy with anything less, but am as the father who awaited the return of his son, unable to enjoy his riches so long as his heart yearned for the wanderer. So I yearn and watch for thee whenever ye turn aside. For as sheep, ye tend to stray away; but My love shall exert a restraining influence, and I shall draw thee back.

Only be sure that ye do not draw back from Me, for I will never coerce thy will. This I have given thee — the power of choice, and the privilege of determining thine own destiny. This I shall never violate. For this reason give I the many warnings: resist not, grieve not, quench not My Holy Spirit; for I have given Him unto thee to continually woo thee unto Myself.

Well I know the instability of the human heart and natural affection. Thus I have supplied My own love to thy heart by the indwelling of My Holy Spirit. He it is who testifies of Me. He it is who prompts thy worship, who kindles the fires of devotion, who constantly draweth thee to Myself. Yea, I have made full provision. I have stated it fully though tersely in My words: Be filled with the Spirit, and ye shall not be left open to the danger of being drawn away from Me by the desires of the carnal nature. (Gal. 5:16) For the carnal nature is hostile toward God, but the Holy Spirit within you ever crieth 'Abba, Father', and He shall glorify Me at all times. (Gal. 4:6, Jno. 16:14)

Do ye long to love Me more deeply? Seek the infilling of My Holy Spirit. Do ye long to serve with greater ardor? Seek the infilling of the Holy Spirit. Prayest thou for a greater burden for the lost? Seek a fresh anointing of My Spirit. Long ye for a more fervent prayer life? O, be filled with the Spirit! Has the world made inroads into thy heart and mind? Have the cares of this world brought anxiety and robbed thee of thy peace and joy? Again I say to thee: *Be filled with the Spirit.*

In this one magnificent gift, I have made full provision for thine every need. Narrow down thy prayers. Seek only to be filled; and in the overflow every other need shall be met. Yea, every desire shall be spontaneously fulfilled. For the will of God shall be accomplished through thy yielded vessel, and it is written, 'He that doeth the will of God abideth forever.' (I Jno. 2:17b) This is My highest will for thee: that ye be yielded to and filled with the Spirit, and that ye walk in the liberty and the power of the Spirit . . . unctionized, prompted, led, illumined, vitalized by the indwelling life of God.

Let thy stimulation be of the Spirit. Let the love of God rule and overrule thine every action and thine every word.

> *"Would you live for Jesus, and be always pure and good?*
> *Would you walk with Him within the narrow road?*
> *Would you have Him bear your burden,*
> *   carry all your load?*
> *Let Him have His way with thee."*
>
> —*Nusbaum*

I Will Not Keep Silent

My lips shall speak forth Thy praise.
  Yea, my tongue is the pen of a ready writer. (Psa. 45:1)
My mouth shall be filled with the wonders of Thy greatness,
    and I shall magnify Thy Name.
In the midst of the people shall I lift up my voice and worship
    Thee.
  I will not keep silent;
For if I keep silent, my soul is consumed within me.
O Lord God, what unbearable desolation would be ours if Thou
    didst not speak to us!
  How our hearts cry out for an answer from Thee:
Surely Thy heart likewise longeth for a response from us!
I will not keep back that gift which only I can give:
    my praise, my worship, my adoration.
I love Thee, I will extol Thee unashamedly before the multitude.
  I will not withhold this from Thee,
      though surrounded by the callous and the unconcerned.
  This belongeth unto Thee. This will I give to Thee.
As it is written: Render to man the things of man, but
      give unto God that which is His rightful due.

(Matt. 22:21)

*   *   *

By Silence Ye Rob Me of My Glory

Yea, My child, I have been betrayed more times by silence than
by words.

By words a man may sin against Me, but by silence do ye rob
Me of My Glory.

Said I not, if those who praised kept silent, I would cause
the stones to testify?

Yea, but I take no pleasure in the stones, but I rejoice in My
people.

For I have made the stones and have made them truly
to witness of Me;

but My children have I borne; yea, they are flesh of My flesh —
bone of My bone.

How much have we to share!

It is as we work together that My will is accomplished.

I am continually placed on trial in the eyes of men by the
enemy.

Ye are My defense.

For as I plead thy cause before the throne against the devil's
accusations,

so I depend upon you to defend Me before those who cast
doubts and aspersions upon Me before men.

Truly these words are prompted of the devil the same
as the words he brings to Me against you.

Never miss an opportunity to uphold Me;

and know this: as ye testify of Me and plead My cause
before men,

I will surely plead thy cause and witness for thee before
the Father.

But as it is written;

if you are ashamed of Me before men, I will be ashamed of you
when I stand before the Father in your behalf.

(Mk. 8:38)

Thy Grace Hath Overflowed

O Lord, my heart is melted in the midst of me,
>for Thou hast laid Thine hand upon me,
>and I know not what Thou doest.

I am an uncomely vessel of clay,
>yet hast Thou filled me with Thy glory.

Yea, my breath is gone out of me,
>and my thoughts are lost in amazement.

Thou art both at once power and tenderness;
>majesty and humbleness; righteousness and compassion.

Thou movest at the same time with swiftness and with patience;
>with severity and with mercy.

Thy love hath altogether overwhelmed me.
>Thy grace hath overflowed me and engulfed me
>>as the billows of the mighty deep.

Thou dost continually encompass my path.
>In my going out and my coming in,

Thou pourest out Thy Spirit in a flood upon me,
>and from the deeps within me,

Thou art as a fountain gushing forth and filling all my being.

The Spirit of Life

O My child, drink deeply of My Spirit, and check Me not,
>for I give not My Spirit by measure; neither shall My words
>>fail.

Only receive Me freely;
for as thou receivest, even so can I give,
and I long to fill thee continually, yea, I desire to make thee
a fruitful branch.
Thou canst bear no fruit of thyself.
Only when My life is flowing *through* thee canst thou impart life
to others.
Heed not the voice of the adversary;
for he is a murderer from the beginning
and seeketh thy destruction,
and worketh death continually.
Rebuke him in My Name.
Resist not My Spirit, and set not a limit upon My movings.
Yield Me complete control, and hold not back,
and thou shalt break forth and yield an hundredfold.
My Spirit is the Spirit of Life, and I am in Thee and upon
thee that thou shouldst not be barren nor unfruitful;
and whomsoever thou touchest in faith shall feel My quicken-
ing power.
Life shall rise out of death; yea, Eternal Life out of spiritual
death.
Is this not even greater than My servant Lazarus?
For I said, 'Greater works than I do shall ye do, because I go
unto My Father.' (Jno. 14:12)
The world seeth me not — but ye see me, and because
I live, ye shall live also.
And thy life shall quicken those whom thou touchest.
For I am not the God of the dead, but the God of the
living.
And thou truly livest only as Christ liveth in thee.
Only limit Me not through blind unbelief.
For faith layeth hold upon those things which are not
and lo, they become realities.
By My Spirit, Life springeth forth from death,
for I am the Resurrection and the Life.
Lay hold upon My Greatness.
Utilize My Power, for My Power is infinite,
and My grace surpasses human comprehension.

Open thou the eyes of faith,
    and thou shalt be astonished at those things which I shall do,
        for the time is short,
        and much remains to be accomplished.
Waste not thy life by endeavoring to walk in thine own strength.
Abandon thyself unreservedly to Me,
    and reckon not the outcome.
Have no concern as to the reception of men;
    for I will receive thee, and I will reward thee,
    and all else shall perish.
Though thou shouldst walk alone, I will be thy comfort and
            satisfaction.
        My love for thee is deep and constant.

*   *   *

O Lord, make Thou my love for Thee even so.
    For I love Thee as I have never loved another;
    and I would love all others as Thou hast loved me.
Let me gather Thee in mine embrace,
    for Thy love consumeth me altogether.
For such love as Thine, I would gladly lay down my life.
    O let me never fail Thee. Hold Thou me up.
    Yea, keep me from stumbling, and present me faultless
        before Thy throne with joy.

The Fountainhead

Holy Father, I come to Thee. Where else is there to go? Thou art the soul's home. Thou art of all life the one fountainhead. Thou art the source of all true peace. Thou art the sole dispenser of all true joy.

Who has been Thy counselor and from whom hast Thou sought advice? Surely Thou art the all-wise God and in Thee is resident wisdom to solve every mystery, and nothing is hid from Thy sight. No darkness can abide Thy light. Thou hast the answer to every problem, the solution to every perplexity. I may rest in knowing this and be assured that Thou art working out all things in accordance with Thy sovereign plan.

Or I may set myself to learn the answers; to know Thy mind and will in times when this knowledge is necessary. Teach me, Lord, when to simply trust and when to seek understanding.

That He May Heal

O My child, hast thou ever sought Me in vain? Hast thou ever truly called that I gave not answer? Have ye ever knocked that I did not open? Surely I have invited thee and I have encouraged thee. Yea, I am as eager to share with thee as ye are in need of wisdom. I am as ready to extend to thee My help as ye are desirous to have Me do so.

Knowest thou not that I am in thee and thou art in Me? Said I not that I am the Vine and ye are the branches? How could I more clearly have indicated our oneness in operation? I mean ye not to labor on in the heat of the day until life's span be finished whilst I look down upon thee, watching from some distant point. Ye need not call as though ye sought for Me to send outside help from afar off. Nay! I am *in thee*. I am *with thee*. I am *thy life*. Not simply *the* life, but thy very life. LIVE ME. Yield thyself to Me, and I will direct thy goings.

My Word shall be thy strength. My Word is a quickening, powerful agency. Use it! Use it much. Use it often. Use it always. Use it upon thine own soul and spirit to distinguish what is of the Spirit and what is of thine own personality. Use it upon the thoughts and intents of thy heart to discover what is of divine wisdom and insight and what is of the vain imagination of the old carnal nature. Yes, use it upon thyself; and as ye do so, ye shall be able to remove the beams from thine own eye and shall then see clearly to remove the motes from thy brother's eye.

The more thou shalt wield the Sword of My Word upon thine own proud flesh, the more ye shall sharpen thy faculties to use it with deftness upon others. Never presume to reverse the order, for as a novice ye may kill rather than cure. My Word is Spirit and Life. I give it to quicken, not to destroy.

But I would not have you ignorant of the devices of Satan. For he maketh himself to appear as an angel of light. He feareth not to use the scripture; but he useth it as an instrument of death. He maketh the truth of God a lie. He useth it with evil intent to destroy.

But My Spirit worketh in love. As it is written, 'He bruiseth that He may heal'. I discipline that ye may know My concern for you as a Father. And when I use the sword, I use it for thine edification and correction. No chastening is painless, but afterward it is profitable. Resist Me and thy life is in jeopardy. Live in Me as the branch in the vine, and let My life flow through thee, constantly flowing back and forth . . . My life to thee and thy life to Me, and there shall be less need for pruning.

Unfinished Tasks

My Father, I am not capable of doing all those things that are demanded of me in the course of a day. For every task completed, numerous other needful duties are left undone. This is not a complaint that life is over-burdensome, but rather a cry to Thee for understanding, and for wisdom to improve the situation: how to reach the end of the day with a feeling of some degree of satisfaction in a job well done. It is not restful to, as it were, sleep on loose ends — to be forever uncomfortably aware of the multitudinous tasks still waiting.

For as time passes, so much of what we have failed to accomplish can no longer be done at all. Surely there must be enough time and enough strength provided to do the vitally essential things. Dear Father, I not only fail to accomplish the task, but lose my sensitivity to Thy guidance, and in doing this, I soon have also lost the joy I would have had if I had pleased Thee.

Give Me the Firstfruits

O My child, *do not bring Me the unfinished tasks.* There will always be work to do. This also can be a snare of the enemy; for he would deceive you into feeling that all work is worthy in itself — that simply to be occupied is good. This is not true.

To sit still, yes, even to have recreation, is sometimes just as important and ofttimes more so. If ye were a hundred people, ye would discover that ye would have a hundred times more unfinished tasks!

Give Me a heart that has learned how to become quiet and to rest. Anybody can work. Few people know how to be quiet. Being quiet is not being lazy. Most lazy people are never truly quiet. Those who do the least, frequently talk the most, and are seldom able to be still and collect their wits.

Ye *must* be able to collect yourself — to take time to absorb the Spirit of God. For to be freshly-filled with the Spirit will bring the guidance and direction and wisdom, *and the will* to do His bidding. The purpose of spending time with God is more than simply enjoying His presence: It is to fit you for the labors next at hand. The Mount of Transfiguration was not a separate play from the deliverance of the demoniac. It was the first scene. Christ's words to the impotent disciples leave us in no doubt as to this. (Mk. 9:1-29)

So come to Me, as I have so often invited thee to do — heart open, hands uplifted and *empty*. Don't bring Me your work. Bring Me yourself. It is *you* that I love, not your enterprises. The more you draw near to Me in singleness of heart, the clearer will be your guidance on life's pathway, and the less danger there will be of your substituting human activities for Spirit-directed ministries.

Keep your heart tender, lest your work become destructive.

Lion of Judah

With a great deliverance, O God, Thou hast brought my soul out of bondage. With what abundance of mercy and love hast Thou redeemed and justified, cleansed and forgiven! I was bowed down as a bond slave in the galley of despair, but Thine eye was upon me to deliver, and Thy love was toward me to lift me up, and Thine hand Thou hast stretched forth to set me free.

Lo, what complete liberation in Thy presence! What a healing power in the sunshine of Thy love! What blessing in the very thought of Thy kindness! My heart melteth at the contemplation of Thy mercy and Thy grace!

O Divine Redeemer! Blessed, holy Lamb of God! Jesus, my Saviour! My constant Companion. The I Am. The ever-present, all-powerful One! Lion of Judah breaking chains asunder, setting captives free. Lamb of God, by Thy shed blood washing away every stain of sin.

The Broadening View

Behold I will be to thee more than thy mind can grasp. For as I said to My disciples, 'I have many things to tell thee but ye cannot bear them now'. (Jno. 16:12) I have many glorious facets of truth to reveal to thee, but ye are not able to receive them all at once. For it is written, the light was not given to be hid. The truth of God as contained in the Holy Scriptures was given that it might be revealed. (Mk. 4:22) Whatever truths may be obscure to thee now, I am anxiously waiting to make plain.

So give thyself to diligent study — yea, search the Scriptures for they are given for the purpose of revealing Me. What joys await! It shall be as when one ascends a mountain, and from each successively higher vantage point he thrills at an increasingly broadening view. So shall it be; and I will take thee progressively higher via the written Word until that day when ye shall see Me face to face! Then shall ye know Me and understand Me even as I now know you. Glorious consummation!

As
a
Dove

O my Father, I would pour out my soul unto Thee.

I am unworthy of all Thy benefits and dull of hearing. Thy teachings I treasure, and to be instructed of Thee is my desire, but I sit too seldom at Thy feet, and my heart is too often occupied with other affairs.

Thy Spirit oft would settle as a dove upon my shoulder, but my activity affords Him no quiet resting-place. Inspiration Thou wouldst bring to me, but my thoughts are preoccupied with the cares of this life. Deliver me from the snare of the fowler . . . from any contrivance of circumstances that would seek to destroy the ministry of the dove of peace in my heart.

Give to me a quiet, meditative spirit that will provide fertile soil for the propagation of Thy Truth. Let me be open to an encounter with Thee at all times. Separate from me all that is evil, and let me cling stedfastly to all that is good.

Be my instructor; be my guide, and withhold not Thy rod of correction when Thou discernest that I have need of rebuke. My hope is in Thee, for I am unable to order my own steps wisely, neither can I escape the pitfalls except Thy Spirit protect me and keep me.

I will trust in Thee. I will lean my entire weight upon Thee. I will reckon on Thy mercy and depend upon Thy power.

*　　　　*　　　　*

There Need Be No Cross-purposes

Thou art less concerned than I about thy welfare. I am deeply interested in every phase of thy life. I know the perplexities — the complexities — the tendency toward disintegration. I am omnipresent and omniscient. There are these elements present within thee also, because of the presence of My Spirit.

In Christ all things are drawn (or held) together. All of life, when His power is operative in a life, tends toward unification and singleness of purpose. Albeit, at the same time, while this first is true, it is also true that through thee I am reaching out to know, to do, and to be in other places and other lives. Do not be perplexed by this. Continue with Me, and I will show thee how these two forces can work together and complement each other.

They may seem to be in conflict, but this is not the case. They are opposites, but they are not incompatible. They are going in two different directions, but moving to a common goal.

Ye may not understand now, but I will show you later. Let it bring peace to your heart now, to know that I am in both. Let them pass each other, as the planets move in their orbits . . . silently, beautifully. There need be no collision nor cross-purposes. It is all by My Spirit, saith the Lord.

Rest it with Me. I will bring the clarification.

Out of the Depths

Unto Thee, O God, do I cry; unto Thee do I lift up my voice.
Hear me from the deeps; for out of great depths do I cry.

Be Thou near to me, and lift me out of the darkness. Yea,
raise me to Thy bosom and let Thy light surround me.

For surely the battle is Thine.
This warfare with the enemy is verily the conflict of the ages.

For we wrestle not against flesh and blood,
neither can we in our own strength offer any resistance.
Come to our aid. Be Thou our strength in our weakness.

By the power of Thy Spirit, make us to stand.

For we are Thy people. We are called by Thy Name.
Let us not be ashamed, neither let the enemy put us to confusion.
In the thick of the battle, let the shout of victory be heard.
Let us rise up and praise Thee though the battle be hot against us.

For Thou, our God, art a Mighty Man of War.

Rise up in our behalf and set up a counter-attack,
yea, beseige the enemy and bring his power to nought.

The Glory of My Presence

Hear, saith the Lord, and give Me audience.
I will speak words of comfort and words of cheer to My people.

Mine eyes behold, and Mine ears are open, and lo,
    all through the night have I stood watch.
Through the darkness have I set limits for thy protection,
    and lo, the enemy cannot break through the lines.
        For I have set a limit to his power,
        and I have curtailed his activities.
I am in the midst of My people to give them peace.
    I shall dine with them at the table,
        though countless hosts encamp round about.
I shall cover them with My almighty hand,
and the glory of My presence shall rest upon them,
and my light shall shine throughout their midst.
Lo, the eyes of the enemy shall not be able to bear the sight.
      My peace I give unto you:
    not as the world giveth, give I unto you.
Let not your heart be troubled, neither let it be afraid.

(Jno. 14:27)

Reign Supreme

O Blessed Saviour, in Thy Name we are mighty
  to the pulling down of strongholds.
Thy Name hath power to put the enemy to flight.
Though it be precious to the hearts of Thy saints,
  it is fearful to the devil.
For he knoweth Thy power; he recognizeth Thine authority.
  Would that we were equally aware of Who Thou art!
We struggle on through the maze of life
thinking of Thee all too often in merely sentimental ways.
We sing of Thee as our Friend, and even in this,
we ascribe to Thee little more than we think of in regard to
our earthly friends, and sometimes even less.
  We find it easier to clasp the hand of a friend
    than to experience the reality of Thy presence.
We find it more simple to discuss our problems with some dear
one than to pour them out to Thee with confidence that Thou art
indeed listening to us . . . not to mention our failure (or fear)
to wait for Thy response.
Thus when we should be 'coming to the garden alone' to walk
and talk with Thee, we are substituting earthly companionship
for heavenly — the seen for the unseen — whilst we continue
to sing of Thee as our friend.
What do we know of Thee as the God of Elijah on Mt. Carmel?
Or as the God who brought more than two million Israelites out of

the bondage of Egypt with not one body afflicted with sickness?
Or the God who spread His protecting wings over every individual who was sheltered by the blood in the night when
the death angel passed through the land?
Do we know Thee as the Shunamite who cried "It is well" in the
face of death and soon after took her child up alive? —
Or are we instead like Martha, content to await the final day of
resurrection?
Have we sung "Come Almighty to deliver, Born to set Thy people
free" and been content with poetic beauty of mere words?

O Lord, our God, and our Blessed Saviour, may we re-evalu-
ate our personal status in our relationship to Thee.
May there be born in our hearts a more mature concept of Thee—
Immanuel — God with us.
God—not altered nor hewn down to our own size and limitations—
The One before whom Satan went away disappointed and
demons fled at the sound of His voice and trembled at the
thought of His Name.
Yes, "His Name is Wonderful". Teach us O God, to use it as we
have been given the privilege to do.
For the Kingdom of God is not in *this place* or in *that place*.
Lo, the Kingdom of God is within us!
Reign there supreme over our affections and emotions.
Let Thy will be done in our hearts as it is done in heaven.
And let Thy Name be to us a weapon in prayer to bind the powers
of the enemy and to release those whom he has bound.
Let it be so *now*, that when Thou comest we may have tro-
phies to lay at Thy feet.

—Amen.

A World Within a World

My child, I am near to thee; yea, I am with thee and in thee
and round about thee. Yea, we are in truth one—even as I prayed

on earth, that as I was in the Father and the Father in Me, so also those whom the Father gave Me, My own chosen dear ones, might be one in us. One in heart. One in thought. One in desires and motives. Yea, one with us by virtue of their having been separated from the course and fashion of this present evil world and joined in a new and holy fellowship in the Eternal.

Not taken out of the world, thus removing the need of continual consecration, but left in the midst of conflicting spiritual forces and given strength to maintain purity of heart, and endued with power from on high, fortified by the gift of the abiding presence of the Holy Ghost, who though unseen becometh a more telling influence than the atmosphere of the world. So thou art become a world within a world even as the atom is a world of its own within the outer molecule.

Be Thou
My Door
of Hope

Out of the depths have I cried unto Thee. Hear me, O God, for my heart longeth for Thee more than the hart that seeketh the waterbrook. Except Thou be my comfort, my heart dwelleth in silence. Except for Thy companionship, my soul wandereth in solitude. But Thou art not far from me. Thy loving kindness shall gather me again. Thou wilt reveal Thyself to me in Thy tenderness and nearness.

Thou art gracious and full of compassion, yea, it is written, 'His mercies are fresh every morning and great in His faithfulness'. (Lam. 3:23) And again, 'His heart is touched by the feeling of our infirmities, and He is acquainted with our grief'. (Heb. 4:15)

Be Thou my help, for to whom else shall I go? Be Thou my Door of Hope, for darkness is round about me.

My Energizing Spirit

O My child, I will help thee, and that speedily. I am nearer to thee than breathing. I am more real than all thy desires or thy fears. Yea, My Spirit is a quickening, life-giving Spirit. The letter killeth — the law condemns, but I say unto thee, I come to forgive; I come to restore; I come to bless and to heal. I come to be thy Light.

In My presence there is no darkness. Have ye not read that in the Eternal City there is no need of candle, nor of the sun or moon, because the Lamb is the Light of it? Surely if I can brighten all of Eternity, I have ample supply to flood thy heart and mind and thy body with My mighty power, My light, and My love — My deep joy and My energizing Spirit. Have ye not read (Rom. 8:11) that the self-same Spirit that raised the body of Jesus up from the dead *dwelleth in YOU* to energize your mortal body through His indwelling Spirit? Ye need not depend upon thine own limited strength and endurance.

My arm is not shortened that it cannot save. I stand ready to support thee. Yea, to thee I say, *underneath are My everlasting arms.* They are not only powerful arms, but they are arms of love and tenderness.

When ye think of Me, disassociate thy thoughts from all that ye know of people, for I am Infinite. Think of it! In all My characteristics, I am not only far beyond all that ye could ever appropriate or need, but beyond all ye can even fancy.

Not in wildest imagination can ye guess the depths of My love. By no mental gymnastics can ye compute My power. Never mind! Just give Me thy hand and I will give thee Myself. Give Me every doubt, every fear, every heartache. I am here to help. I am here to carry thy load and minister to thy need. I will not fail thee nor forsake thee. I am thy God; be not afraid.

Rest Thy Case In My Hands

Behold, I am thy God, and I am with thee to help thee.
  In the darkness I will be to thee a light,
and when thou walkest alone, I will be thy companion.
  Have I spoken, and will I not bring it to pass?
Have I promised and will I not perform it?
  Yea, I will surely do all that I have said.
  For My hand shall be upon thee.
When thou wakest and when thou sleepest,
  I shall be ever at thy right hand,
    and I shall give thee strength.
For thou art My child, and thy needs are My constant care.
Therefore I have asked thee to roll thy burdens and thine
    anxieties upon Me,
for every circumstance which toucheth thee is My concern.
      Yea, I am not only concerned,
but I am able to deliver thee and I *will* deliver thee
  as surely as thou shalt rest thy case in My hands.
  Let not care lay its head upon thy heart,
  but lay thou thine head upon My shoulder,
and I will bear thee up, and I will surely bring thee peace.
  For He that keepeth thee neither slumbers nor sleeps.
Yea, the Lord thy God is thy strength,
  and in Him is no weariness.

He tireth not at thy coming,
and thy cry is welcome to His ears however frequent.

Cast thyself upon His mercies,
for His lovingkindness never faileth,

and His grace and compassion are inexhaustible.
His faithfulness is extended to all generations.

My Help Is In Thee

Lord God, thou art *my* God: my help is in Thee.

Thou wilt never leave me nor forsake me.

Thou wilt bring me through,

and I shall praise Thy Name!

Thy
God
Forever

Behold, I am Thy God forever. In thy going out and in Thy coming in, I am with thee. In the time of trouble, I will be thy strong defense, and in the hour of need, I am thy sure habitation.

Mine eye is ever watchful and I shall undertake for thee according to My glorious riches. Is it not written: 'the very hairs of your head are all numbered'? (Matt. 10:30) Surely My love for thee is altered by no external circumstances. Never look there to determine My pleasure nor reckon My displeasure by untoward providence. It is only the one who allows the cloud to come between who finds My smile hidden. Keep providence in its place, and My smile will always be observable.

I am the Lord Thy God that changeth not, neither grows weary nor irritable. *My love is constant.* Hold to this one thing. Hold to it as a babe holds to its mother's breast. Hold to it as a drowning man to the life preserver. Hold to it as the needle holds to the pole.

I shall not fail thee nor forsake thee nor disappoint thee in any way. Set thine eye upon the goal, neither allow the incidental things to distract thine attention. The Father knoweth what things ye have need of.

The Ultimate Fulfillment

Blest hand that holds my destiny! Thou art the beginning and the ending: Thou art the giver of all that is satisfying. Thou art the ultimate fulfillment of all man's searching. Anything less leaves the heart still hungry. Anything more is superfluous!

A World of Bliss

O my Father, Thou hast crowned my life with blessings. The half of Thy goodness have I never told. Thou art gracious, and Thy compassion is so deep that even my worst sins have not shut me off from Thy mercy and forgiveness. How hast Thou loved, to redeem one so unworthy! Make my heart to beat with gratitude, nor ever cease praising Thee. Glorious is Thy Name and Thy salvation how great! With Thee is life and through the atoning work of Christ, Thou hast opened to me a world of bliss and a peace that passeth understanding.

My Name Upon Thy Lips

O My child, My arm is about thee to bear thee up, and My right hand under thy head. I will hold thee fast and sustain thee though trouble break upon thee as a mighty flood. Let My Name be upon thy lips, for it is powerful. Do not count the cost.

A Teachable Spirit

Hearken unto the voice of the Lord and give thyself diligently to keep His commandments. Each day ye are confronted with opportunities to minister. I would have you be a sharp instrument with which I can thresh the mountains. (Isa. 41:15) In order for this to be true, ye must have hearing ears and ye must have an obedient spirit.

It is not enough that ye have come to know Me in a salvation experience, for this is only the beginning. Ye have been chosen for a purpose, and I cannot use you in the fulfillment of this purpose unless ye submit thyself to My training and teaching.

As in the days of old, I am looking for disciples to be used ultimately as leaders. Many there were who followed, as it is written, because of the miracles performed, but few there were who sought Me with a true desire to be taught, to receive My words, and to put My teachings into practice.

Bring Me an obedient heart, a teachable spirit, and a mind ready to learn. I shall be able then to make of thee a disciple and to bring thee at last into a position of responsibility. The cost is high, but the rewards shall be gratifying; but ye shall not be aware of either the cost nor the rewards because the joy of fellowshipping closely with Me shall so occupy thy heart.

Purify My Desires

Lord Jesus, make me a learner. All Thou hast said is true, and I long to be not a follower only, but a genuine disciple. I am reminded that the disciple must take up his cross, and must do so daily. A disciple cannot turn back, nor can he be torn between conflicting loyalties. Thou hast made the requirements stringent and hast set the standard very high. I may wish to attain and yet fail.

I may desire to enter into discipleship and be rejected. Let it not be so, Lord, for lack of love for Thee. Let it not be for want of zeal or consecration. Let it not be on account of the love of the world and its pleasures.

Purify my desires until I want nothing but Thee alone, and seek nothing but to bring Thee joy.

Turn my apathy to empathy, and change my longings to firm resolves.

Strengthen my hand to do right, and remove swiftly all that weakens.

My Presence Shall Go With Thee

Come unto Me all ye that are weary in body and tired of soul, and I will refresh thee and renew thine energies and give thee fresh zeal and new courage. I will not fail thee.

In the hour of need I will surely, undertake for thee. I will not disappoint Thee. I will support thee and comfort thee and will keep thee from all evil.

Though darkness press about thee, lo, I Myself will be Thy victory. Yea, My presence shall go with thee, and I will give thee peace.

Guide and Guard Us

Blessed Father, precious Lamb of God, tender, loving, gracious Holy Spirit! What encouragement in the very thought of Thee! What strength in but the breathing of Thy Name! What balm to the weary soul in the sweet consciousness of Thy presence!

No heart can stay distressed except it remain outside Thy love. No turmoil of soul can persist when brought under the influence of Thy peace.

So hold us, O God, within the circle of Thy loving arms. Grant us Thy wisdom for the daily tasks. Give us Thy direction in decisions, and so regulate our thoughts that we may move under the guidance of Thy divine and perfect will, and thus be guarded against selfishness and rebellion and unsanctified strategy.

The Shepherd Speaks Gently

My little one, hast thou not heard My word, go not into the bypaths? Lo, I, thy loving Shepherd am by thy side. Why shouldst thou wander off? I have brought thee into tender, green pastures and beside a flowing stream. Let thy soul drink deeply, and feed to thy heart's content.

It is no idle pastime: I have brought thee here for My own good pleasure, and for purposes only known to Me. In the days ahead thou shalt know why we came this way. Trust Me now and be unmoved by any disturbance. The distant call thou shalt ignore. Stay close to Me, and thy heart shall delight in thy God. Thy fellowship with Me shall be precious beyond anything words can tell. I love thee deeply, and when love is deep, words are little needed. Shouting is unthinkable. Devotion is silent and love silences conversation. The shepherd speaks gently, and lambs do not respond to shouts. He who yells at the sheep is behaving like an hireling rather than like a shepherd. He shall bring confusion. The inner ear of the spirit is attuned to hear the still, small voice.

Lay thine head upon My knee and let Me quiet thee. Forget all the rest. What others do need not concern thee. I have never required thee to understand the actions of others. Make it no concern of thine. Only yield. Let Me do all the rest.

Sleep is My love gift to thee. Do not despise it nor set it aside. Rest in My care, for I love to care for thee but I cannot when ye are wrongfully anxious about the behaviour of others. I will correct them and minister to them Myself, for I also love them just as I love you. But they are too occupied to come to Me now. Leave them *all* to Me, and come, rest in My arms.

Prayer Response

Blessed Jesus, my soul cries out to Thee in response to Thy love. I would rather come to Thee than build ten cities. No accomplishment brings the joy and deep satisfaction that comes from being near Thee and feeling my hand in Thine.

Loving Saviour, blessed be Thy Name!

The Spirit Requireth Not Language

O my Father, how can I express that which Thou dost work within my heart? My soul has no language to speak except in groanings that are too deep and mysterious to articulate.

Give me Thy wisdom and understanding in like fashion, so that even without words from Thee I may know what thou doest, even as without words I know what I feel. Surely the Spirit requireth not language, but heart with heart may commune. Perhaps it is possible to fellowship in this manner in a union deeper than the level of communication by speech. For this I thank Thee.

Spiritual Communication

Yes, My child, there are times when words are an impediment to the flow of the Spirit as rocks are to a stream. Ye have become accustomed to the verbal expression of thought when communicating with other persons, but there is a quality and a depth of union possible in the Spirit where words are totally useless: Ye shall find it so in Heaven. Talking, as ye know it on earth, shall be conspicuous by its absence. Little need be said when understanding is perfect. This is one reason why those who have progressed the farthest toward truly saintly lives have become extremely sparse with words, while the worldly man or woman is garrulous and freely talkative.

As ye seek this spiritual concourse ye shall discover a rich interplay from soul to soul and new experiences of spiritual communication, plus a new area of ministry. Wait upon Me. I shall teach you more about this.

Divine
Timing

My times are governed by My wisdom. When I speak to thee, directing thy way, obey speedily. There are time elements involved that are vital. As pieces of a jigsaw puzzle fit but one way, so My providences work out with accurate and precise detail, and perfect timing is very essential. Doing right can cause dire calamity if carried out at the wrong time. An illustration of this principle would be proceeding down a highway and disregarding traffic signals. The direction of travel and the destination may be correct, but the time element being wrong would prevent a safe arrival. Never disregard My signals no matter how lofty may be your motivation.

I will never be late, so ye need not move in undue haste. Nay, and I would not be premature so as to bring even a blessing before the time when it can be properly and joyfully received.

So learn to be very sensitive to My timing and move when I speak, however softly that may be. Ye shall be thrilled and encouraged with the increase of fruitfulness in thy ministries.

Sensitivity

Blessed be Thy Name, Father. All my life I have watched Thy time clock and have been blessed to see Thy love and wisdom combined. If I have grown less sensitive, restore whatever has been lost, and bring me to a place where I shall see far greater things than those in the past.

Mark my path clearly, and give me sharp eyes and ears and an obedient will.

The Lord Is At the Door

The time is short, and the hour is late, and darkness is coming upon the earth. Lo, the Lord is at the door.

Go not in the path of folly. Walk not in carelessness. For in spite of all the warning signals there is a spirit of levity which hath taken hold of many, and they do not seek My face. Lo, when ye ought to be occupied with prayers and fastings and repentance ye are busily engaged in that which is frivolous and of no lasting value.

How long shall I bear with you? O My people, how shall I stay My hand of punishment?

Forsake thy sins and return from thy backslidings, that I may have mercy upon thee and forgive and restore thee, and use thee in the place where ye are so sorely needed.

Be reconciled to Me quickly and set thy face like a flint to seek to know My perfect will. Hear no voice but Mine, and be so yielded to Me that ye will never draw back regardless of any cost.

Be ready to act as My ambassador. Lo, I have important messages for thee to carry. I may send you to strangers and to places foreign to thee. That is My prerogative. I ask of thee once again only obedience. Study obedience that it may have deeper significance to thee. Then *walk* in the light revealed.

Surely I will be with thee. I am thy God, and ye shall be My messenger.

Prayer Response

Blessed Jesus, I would worship Thee alone, and I would serve none other.

I would hear Thy voice and would do Thy bidding.

I am not wise, but I trust Thee to give wisdom. I am not faithful, but I look to Thee and depend on Thee for the strength to bring me through the tests.

Be near, and let me rest upon Thy shoulder if ever weariness overtake me. Be my strength and I shall gladly serve Thee.